Mediterranean Vegetarian Diet

The Basic Facts to Start a Balanced
Vegetable Food Diet

70 Mouth-Watering Recipes for Cooking Eggs and
9 Diets Health

By
Kimberley Smith

Cover by Seksak Kerdkanno on Pixabay

[Free for commercial use - No attribution required]

Visit the author's page

Write to: kimb.smith.books@gmail.com

OTHER PUBLICATIONS BY KIMBERLEY SMITH:

Raising Chickens For Eggs:

The Beginner's Guide To Building A Chicken-Coop, To Learn How to Raise A Happy Backyard Flock. A Homesteading Solution While You Are At Home

Hydroponic Gardening:

A Detailed Guide on Hydronics to Learn the Principles Behind Gardening and Build a Wonderful System While at Home. Techniques for Your Vegetable Cultivations

Keto Copycat Cookbook Restaurant:

A Keto Diet to Feel Your Best. Easy Recipes for Beginners for All Seasons From Appetizers to Desserts to Reduce Inflammation, Lose Weight, and Heal the Immune System

EASY KETO DESERTS

67 Recipes for Beginners for All Seasons

to Reduce Inflammation, Lose Weight, And Heal the Immune System

A Ketogenic Diet to Feel Your Best

MENS SANA
IN CORPORE
SANO

Sommario

Vegetarianism and raw food

Let us first examine the proper and etymological meaning of the word vegetarianism.

Derived from the verb vegetate, it serves to define that lifestyle considered to be the most rational for making the human body vegetarian.

Therefore, it is not limited only to the nourishment of the latter, but to everything that contributes to the perfect success of its vegetative process.

To a regime of life of an ethical and prophylactic nature equally pure and in harmony with the laws of Nature.

Man, through centuries of prejudice and abuse, has transpired the true origin of him who is eminently fugacious as his teeth also testify.

The slow atavistic degeneration that has ensued has meant that his maximum life span, which (as recognized by science) should reach 130 years, reaches just half an average.

It is a mistake to believe that he can no longer go back and restore his original regime without suffering at least momentary disturbances.

Maybe the transition from a carnivorous regime to a strictly vegetarian one, with only cooked

vegetables, can cause transient and never serious disturbances, but the transition to a naturalistic, or even better raw, regime is a true liberation and an absolute regenerating purification.

Moreover, due to excessive prudence, it can also be done gradually and progressively.

For man's nourishment, the following basic elements are necessary: proteins, carbohydrates, mineral salts, fats, cellulose, vitamins, etc.

Now Nature lavishes us all this spontaneously and directly from wheat fields to colorful orchards, from verdant vegetable gardens to flowery prairies where the cow and the hen joyfully draw the elements to give us the milk that is surplus to one from the nutrition of its young and the eggs that overabound the other in proportion to its possibilities of brooding.

Man, with the abuse of his freedom of action on animals, has dissociated this power of will from his responsibility of conscience on which he depends.

The best way to live in harmony is, reclaiming the earth by cultivating it and working it constantly and by presiding over it; the beasts, reptiles, and all animals, plants, and herbs of lower evolutionary cycles will not be able to live there, while life will thus be forced to flow in forms of higher evolution; rationally build your homes, take care of the hygiene of your body with maximum cleanliness, laborious life, purely natural food, upright and sober mental conduct, and life through the lower forms of insects,

parasites, microbes, etc., will not be able to develop around you.

By transgressing all these precise and unchanging, and therefore inexorable laws, man has reduced the period of his natural existence and has made each of his bodily life a real burden of ailments.

He has hindered the great plan of evolution, sacrificing the young sensitive lives of the animals, which he must instead perfect and advance.

Medical science, is forced to limit its work to the sole treatment of the ailments already done and we see climatic stations, health resorts, dietary establishments, etc., spring up every moment; all with more or less vegetarian treatments depending on the possibility of readiness to adapt.

However, late repairs can only stop the continuation of the destructive work, and what has been destroyed can no longer be rebuilt.

Therefore, all that remains is to cry the alarm so that we can retrace our steps to regain that long and healthy life, the bearer of happiness, which is the heritage of man.

In the vegetarian, naturist regime, in addition to having healthy and pure food, we find everything that can satisfy the most refined tastes.

A plate of pasta topped with cheese and butter, and some fruit, alone would represent all the

nutrition that man needs; therefore, one should not renounce to pleasure of the table.

The incentive to restore the body, with a sober meal, must coincide with the restoration of the mind.

Thus, the physiological restorative action of the body is not completed, it must not be an end in itself, that is, a gross material enjoyment, but it must be a means to return small new energies to the heart so that the spirit can, through this instrument put in order, make them all flow.

Active vegetative life and thinking spiritual life are the two inseparable expressions of the Spirit who realizes his being in this synthesis.

Although man may fell full, even with a handful of seeds and fruit, he must not give up, when he can, at lunchtime which, even if modest, represents in our life a moment of upright and healthy joy; in which the entire harmony of forces and feelings is restored and exalted.

You cannot eat and assimilate food well if you do not enjoy peace and joy and you cannot be happy if you do not nourish yourself healthily, measuredly with pure foods.

"Mens sana in corpore sano"

The theory of the old biological school advocates that from meat we can draw certain amino acids, while we cannot find them directly in the vegetable

kingdom. *This is refuted by the facts that have always practically proved how man not only could live but lives better only with the products of the earth.*

On the other hand, it is enough to empirically observe that the animals, whose meat has been studied and in whose meat amino acids have been found, are exclusively herbivores.

Now if they can carry out this elaborative process through the food of herbs only, in a better way it will be able to disengage a higher-order organism through a complete naturist diet.

Therefore, the alleged usefulness and even less the alleged need to resort to lazy and degrading parasitism not worthy of the nobility of the human being, both as an ethical individuality and as a biological entity, does not hold up.

What is raw food?

We have entertained ourselves and have provided abundant formulas for all those who, while wanting to make a very useful effort with eliminating necrophagy, still hold and are still attached to all the scaffolding and artificial gear of kitchen, cooks, dishwashers, pots, dishes, banquets, and all that is used for nothing other than to waste money and human activities, which could much more profitably be employed in works useful for the evolutionary ascension of humanity.

But there is an even better way to free yourself not only from the burden of cooking, cooked and feasted but from the efforts to which our organism undergoes to transform and assimilate cooked foods and animal products, even if they are not meat products. It is the regime based on everything that nature offers us, not altered by cooking.

Although many chemical combinations that occur during cooking have not yet been specified, it is certain, however, that in addition to killing some vitamins and diastases, acids, salts, etc. are severely altered and all the vital efficiencies that have now been recognized by science are not only useful but necessary for the regular functioning and immunization of our organism.

Sugar, for example, which in its natural state can be found in fruit, milk, and some roots, combined with acids and salts, is of great nutritional and energetic

value, very easy to be burnt by our body; while after being cooked and neutralized by industry, it becomes so inert that it cannot even be transformed by saccharomyces.

Our organism struggles enormously to reverse it and burn it because it must first reoxidize it with gastric acids to return it in part to the state as it is found in nature.

Often and in the long run, our organism does not have the resources and the strength to carry out this tiring recovery and the neutral sugar passes unnoticed into the blood causing diabetes and other serious imbalances and pathological changes.

Let's see how the tomato, which in its raw state is a dissolver, diuretic, vitalizing, digestive and refreshing; after cooked, on the other hand, it becomes perfectly the opposite, determining uric acids, liver stones, warming form of the viscera and urinary tract, indigestible, and loses all vitalizing power.

These still mysterious powers, of which science has recently come to discover some, are not limited only to these, and we can have proof of them through personal observation.

Let's see for example fish in an aquarium that lives perfectly if the water is constantly renewed with other water drawn from the sea or from a source of the earth, but if you stop this exchange, after 24 hours they begin to deteriorate and then die, even if

you give them some food that can make up for those substances contained in running water.

There is therefore a vitalizing factor in the products of the earth in the living state which is neither substance nor vitamin, nor diastasis, but of equal maximum importance whose nature we do not yet know.

But for now, it is enough for us to know only the effects to be able to regulate our eating behavior and we will call this factor: Biogenin x.

Many illustrious scientists such as the Lehmann's, Cristen, Carton, Bircher, Benner, Bachman, Drews, Haig, Bienstock, Tomson, Gerson, Muësle, and many others, have obtained remarkable results both in terms of therapy and prophylactic prevention against ailments, and in fact, while the healings are innumerable, the resistance as prevention to all diseases (not due to ethical errors) can be said to be absolute.

In this regard, it is good to clarify this distinction.

All the diseases that afflict humanity (which should leave the body only for the serene extinction of old age) come from two great causes: ethical error and dietary error.

They determine the pathological effect both in the person who makes the mistake and in his descendants. The best way to cope with it is the development of individual understanding.

Therefore, it is enough for us to deal with the dietary error, while for the other each one will provide for himself through his own experiences and knowledge.

Our being in harmony with ethical laws and not disturbed by irrational nutrition is perfectly resistant to any external attack.

Distracting his resistances by forcing him to laborious digestions and continued detoxification puts him in conditions of leaving place to the attacks of inferior organic lives, which only in this way can take over and undermine their regular functioning of our organism.

In addition to this, the impossibility of completely freeing oneself from all the toxic substances ingested causes a slow and progressive accumulation of poisons that increases over and over, with the decreasing of the elimination powers as time goes by.

 If some consequences of a mis correct diet can therefore be solved when in younger age, it is fatal it is fatal for the elderly.

With the raw naturist regime in harmony with the so-called ethics, true liberation from all evils is obtained.

We know that the elements necessary for our nutrition are: proteins, hydrocarbons, mineral salts, fats, cellulose, and vital efficiencies (those known under the name of vitamins and diastase) and those

known under the name of biogenous what nature lavishes on us in vegetables, fruit, seeds, milk, and eggs, and hands them to us so skillfully combined, that any modification that man wants to make on them can only damage them.

Therefore, having left the task of elaborating them to nature, all that remains for man is to know how to use them, and even in this, the wise nature gives us the means with the alternatives of the seasons. In any case, we give a schematic picture of the powers of vegetable foods that can be eaten raw, so that the reader can make his own food behavior.

It is good to remind that protein or albumin is commonly called no more than a 1 oz. to 50 per day, what is found in 3,5 oz. in oil seeds or in in a cup of milk or an egg.

Then come the hydrocarbons and fats.

The latter can be increased especially in winter to give more calories, with olive oil and butter.

All the rest, mineral salts, cellulose, and vital efficiencies of all kinds can be found both in seeds and in raw vegetables and fruit.

In my opinion, the very shredding and handling of such things should be avoided.

You see the goat, the rabbit, the gazelle, which refuse even the most tender buds simply because they have been touched by man.

Vegetables bought at the market should be revived in running water, fruit equally, oilseeds, peel them off when eating them, and having good teeth avoid mechanical grinding.

However, for those who still care about going to the table, the portions and the aesthetics of the same, as for those whose dentition no longer helps them to chew the seeds, we suggest some formulas based on which they can make an infinity of them.

The interesting and essential thing is to know that a handful of oilseeds, a handful of cereals or legumes macerated in water and a couple of pounds of assorted vegetables and fruit is all that is not only enough for us to nourish ourselves well, but it feeds us most appropriately. rational, hygienic, and prophylactic.

To make raw food combinations, it is first of all necessary to thoroughly clean both the tools and the vegetables and herbs themselves, which must always be washed with running water.

It is also necessary to have a lemon squeezer, a rasping machine, a grater for oilseeds, a squeezer and grinder, and a mortar, possibly in porcelain.

Specific properties of some vegetables

Sweet almonds, in addition to being a complete food because they contain carbohydrates, proteins, fats, mineral salts, cellulose, and a large number of vital efficiencies, if well peeled by keeping them in

fresh water (never hot because it destroys a large part of vital efficiencies) and well minced, are of a great balsamic and refreshing action for stomach patients (you must avoid bitter ones, which instead are harmful for your health, so you have to taste them one by one).

Plums, even dried ones, macerated in freshwater, are laxative and therefore very suitable for constipation by adjusting the daily quantity according to your body.

Since their action is also refreshing, they can be taken in very large quantities in order to obtain the desired effect without any harmful consequences, as it happens with drugs.

Garlic, in addition to being full of vital efficiencies, while raw is a powerful disinfectant of the gastric passages.

The radishes are excellent dissolvers of stones and urates.

Carrots, like onions, are mineralizing and vitalizing elements per excellence. Parsley has a powerful regulating action on the circulation and replacement of the blood.

Sugary fruits are energetic and refreshing, so when you are very tired it is very suitable to take dates, raisins, bananas, figs, etc., drinking a good almond juice or coconut juice over them.

All the organic acids of fruit are extremely precious as diuretic dissolvents, stimulants, and compensators: the malic acid of the apple, the tartaric acid of the grapes, the citric acid of the citrus fruits, the quinic of the cherries and sour cherries, etc.

They also contain pectin, which transforms the organic juices of the fruits into jelly.

All vegetables, such as spinach, lettuce, etc., and also the roots, in addition to the other mineral salts, also contain sodium chloride (cooking salt) in a proportion sufficient to supply the small losses we have; for which it is necessary to make use of very small doses of cooking salt, even being able to do without it, having proved that salt beyond this small requirement is harmful.

If you eat oil seeds youdo not need cereals, but if you want to add them to meals, you can use them by soaking them in water until they become soft up to the center; then they are rinsed in fresh water, ground in the grinder, and seasoned with shaved roots, chopped vegetables, garlic, onion, oil, and lemon, thus obtaining dishes rich in energy and support for the hardest physical efforts. For mental fatigue, a few raw oilseeds are enough to repair the phosphorus loss.

It is a great mistake to worry about typhus bacilli, meba, or others that can be found in raw vegetables, because the bacilli cannot penetrate

the living tissues of the plants, but only remain outside and therefore are easily eliminated with a good washing.

If you want to do naturism for therapeutic purposes, it is good to completely omit common salt (sodium chloride) and replace it with celery salt.

All raw cucurbits well-chewed or chopped have a special cleansing and refreshing action on the intestinal mucous membranes as well as forming an excellent push move for the expulsion of feces

Description and values of vegetarian foods

Cereals. This family is made up of six grains: wheat, rye, oats, barley, rice, and corn, represents the most important part of human food.

Wheat. It stands at the head of others for its content in gluten, vitamins, nitrogenous substances; carbohydrates and mineral salts. It is actually nourishment of primary importance also for its cheapness.

Bread, which is the best handling of wheat, has been the subject of endless discussions for choosing the best way to work it.

We do not dwell on mentioning the many opinions, almost all of which are extremist, but we only say our opinion on the subject, which lies in a middle way.

Since gluten and vitamins are adherents to the woody integument that covers the grain of wheat, it is recommended to make whole bread (with all the bran) to have all the gluten and all the vitamins.

Now as a little inert mass is useful for the catabolism process and a little less gluten and vitamins do not greatly diminish the nutritional values, we believe that the most convenient is a bread that is not completely made by whole meal, a brown bread, that is, reduced to 82%, exactly what our farmers do, whose centuries-old experience and taste, specialized for the most part on this food, have led them to this proportion.

Pasta. *(another derivative of wheat). With this name, we mean all types of macaroni, spaghetti, lasagna, etc., etc. seasoned in various ways as it is practiced in all countries of the world.*

This excellent and popular food occupies a place of primary importance in vegetarian cuisine, both for its mild cost, suitable for all bags, and its great nutritional value.

Given the infinite variety of flavors to which it can be brought, you can eat it all the days of the year and all the years of life, without ever getting tired.

It is very easy to prepare there is no woman at home who in half an hour does not know how to prepare an excellent dish of dry pasta or soup.

A plate of pasta, topped with cheese and butter or with any sauce, is the complete food par excellence, and cheaper than any other.

Wheat provides it with carbohydrates, gluten, protein, and cellulose, while butter gives it fat and aroma, and cheese another protein which, combined with that of wheat, completes it by the difference of specific characters, also giving it another kind of vivifying and energetic elements and completing its flavor.

The variation of sauces and condiments alternates the differences of the aforesaid elements thus facilitating their daily digestion.

Its way of cooking it (especially in southern Italy), that is, in a lot water, then separating it from the latter, makes it much lighter, melted, and therefore more digestible; because some salts difficult to be affected by gastric juices are diluted in the water in which it boils, and a certain amount of starchy substances is also released, thus reducing its composition to a more balanced and more assimilable complex.

Pasta is unjustly infamous as a fattening agent, while this power takes it only from the toxic substances of meat and animal fats with which it is seasoned or combined during the meal and of which it is only a vehicle.

You see, for example, all the peasants of Sicily who daily eat pasta seasoned only with olive oil, or cheese, or tomato, without adding or combining it with meat or animal fats; they are all dry temperatures of very strong fiber resistant to the heaviest work under the lash of the sun or the harsh winter.

They do not know what they are: obesity, fatness, while as soon as we go up to the more comfortable classes, where the first luxury you have is to eat a second dish of meat or season the pasta with sausage, minced meat, clams, and animal fats, we immediately see the fatness, obesity and all their serious consequences, settling in those organisms.

Pasta, eaten in the right quantity alone or accompanied by strictly vegetable and raw second courses, is not fattening at all, being assimilated and ready to be replaced due to the ease of digestion; in the same way as pure water cannot be fatty when taken alone on an empty stomach, and which instead becomes fatty if ingested during meals based on meat and animal fats.

By the same fact it becomes its vehicle, increasing the action of fats on the proliferation of fat cells which are always growing, especially with advancing age; in which the necessarily more sedentary life and the natural slowing down of the replacement powers favor these accumulations of fat.

Rye. It comes immediately after wheat due to the nutritional value of its substance and is, however, less rich in starchy matter and with a particularly pleasant taste, it is used to mix with wheat to obtain a lighter, tastier, and more durable bread.

By itself, for the same reasons, it is food for diabetics and sick people, lighter than wheat.

Barley. This cereal, very rich in mucilaginous materials, is excellent for nutritional decoctions, for the convalescents and children.

Because of these qualities, it was always used in family therapy, even as an emollient and laxative, since the time of Hippocrates who prescribed it, especially in his care.

Oat. Both in the form of flour and displacement, as they are widely used in England (Quaker-Oats), it constitutes a food very rich in salts and phosphorus and very easy to digest, so it is indicated for food for children, old people, and of those who work a lot mentally.

It is prepared in puree, in decoction, or soup with milk. Quaker-Oats is now also prepared in Italy in boxes with instructions for use.

Used raw and marinated in water for 12 hours is even better.

Rice. It is the poorest of cereals in nitrogenous substances and the richest in carbohydrates.

It would be a food of great value, but the industrialization of it, to make it white and shiny by decorticating and bleaching, takes away the most important elements: the mineral, diastatic, nitrogenous principles and vitamins, reducing it to a simple dead starch.

Brown rice is now on the market and its use is highly recommended almost like that of wheat.

Corn. It is also an excellent nutrient.

There are regions where the peasants can be said to live on corn only in the form of poultry; in South America, it is used in the form of cornstarch, that is, first roasted and then milled in impalpable flour.

This is the best way to use it because it is dextrinized so it is easier to digest and has a delicious taste, especially in the manufacture of biscotti and sweets.

Spoiled corn causes pellagra.

The eggs. This product that nature lavishes on us with superabundance, since, especially the hen, produces it far beyond its possibilities of reproduction, is evidently destined for human nutrition.

Prepared for the construction of a complete animal organism, it contains all the basic elements for the life of the future organism, so we draw from it in a very small volume, a perfect complex of nutritional, energetic, and vitalizing substances.

Its weight is on average 2 oz. of which, removed the shell, 1,2 oz consist of white and 6 oz. from the yolk.

The egg white contains for the most part proteins, iron, and silica; the red part, instead, is richer in nitrogen materials, phosphorus, lecithin, fats, energy materials, and vitamins. A food of this value must be the restorative basis of convalescents and growing children.

From one to three egg yolks a day constitute a regenerating nourishment par excellence and this maximum number must not be exceeded, which however must always be combined with fruit, vegetables, and seeds.

Legumes. In them, we also find all the constituents of meat with the addition of carbohydrates, mineral salts, vitamins, and other positive substances, while they are free of all the toxic substances that are additionally found in meat.

At the forefront are lentils with 26% albumin and 59% carbohydrates; then the peas with 24% and 62% respectively, then the beans, chickpeas, broad beans, etc.

However, dried legumes, unlike cereals, contain mineral salts, especially in the woody casing, which, due to their being of little soluble nature, can therefore be difficult to digest, causing special flatulence if taken in large quantities and with all the skins.

This does not happen, however, when they are still green, especially peas, which in this state are highly digestible by the most sickly stomachs, as well as being of exquisite flavor.

To help dissolve the insoluble salts of dried legumes, bicarbonate of soda is excellent, putting a pinch of it during cooking, as well as passing them through a sieve, to separate them from the woody integument.

Mushrooms and truffles. It is worth talking about it in isolation because this family of vegetables, so distinctly original in all its characteristics, is also endowed with very marked nutritional values.

They contain from 20 to 25% albumin mixed with abundant mineral salts and cellulose. In a limited volume, they are therefore very useful and deliciously flavored food.

The truffle, however, being very concentrated and expensive, must be used in moderation and only as a condiment.

Regarding mushrooms, there are many poisonous varieties, but the naturalist Nessler states that, since mushroom poison is a soluble narcotic in sodium chloride (kitchen salt) and acetic acid, immersing them for a few hours in a saltwater solution with wine vinegar, the poisonous substances dissolve remaining in the solution. By repeatedly rinsing the mushrooms in freshwater, they would remain perfectly harmless.

He says that he and his family ate the most poisonous qualities treated in this way for an entire month.

In any case, just eat those well-known local qualities or those produced by artificial crops, which are now found everywhere and which are very safe.

All those alleged tests of the little women: that of the coin, the silver fork, etc., are all to be banned because traces of hydrogen sulfide are enough to make the silver blacken, without the mushrooms being poisonous at all, or vice versa, there may be poisonous mushrooms which do not blacken the silver because not containing the aforesaid acid.

The milk. This food, also supplied to us by nature with superabundance, since, especially the cow, produces much more of it than the needs of its calves, it is also of precious importance.

It contains proteins, a sugar called lactose, mineral salts, and vital efficiencies. All in a stable emulsion and therefore very easy to assimilate.

Very rich in calcium, it is a precious food for children by helping bone formation.

For the milk to be in its full nutritional and vitalizing completeness, it must be taken as soon as it is fed, while all its dynamogenic properties and biogenesis are in full efficiency. It must be ensured that the animal is not sick and its udders must be thoroughly cleaned before being milked and so must the milker's hands.

Milk should also be avoided when it contains colostrum, that is in the first days after childbirth, which is easy to recognize by the yellow color it presents.

Boiled milk loses all its vital powers and diastasis, so it remains a stunted food, limited only to casein and butter; it is, therefore, useful, only for cooking, completing it with other ingredients, or for making cheese, or for a partially nutritious drink to be completed with other things in vital efficiency (fruit, vegetables, etc.).

Butter.

Produced from pure cream, or cream, or mozzarella if you prefer, in the raw state it is a very light and digestible fat, because it derives from a stable emulsion, such as milk, and therefore it's very easy to be re emulsified by biliary secretion and then digested immediately.

Without being cooked, it contains large quantities of diastase and vitamins, so it is advisable to use it at the table by putting it in dishes at the time of eating or, better still, eating it on bread as an appetizer or intermediary.

 To take advantage of its vitalizing powers and its aromatic qualities, in addition to the raw state, it must be fresh and pure cream.

The cheese.

It is derived from curdled milk from which the watery part can thus be removed while maintaining, in a compacted mass, all the nitrogenous material emulsified with the butter.

Thus it is also a food very rich in proteins, fat, calcium salts, and abundant diastases.

Creamy or double cream cheeses are excellent and very nutritious because cream removed from other milk was added to the milk before curdling it; then come the whole cheeses, that is, to which no cream has been removed or added, then low-fat cheeses

that are those whose milk has been removed from the cream to make butter.

It goes without saying that the former have a nutritious superiority, that the latter is excellent, and that the thirds can be used for condiments. In all cases, the so-called strong fermented cheeses due to their strong spicy taste are to be outlawed.

The fermentation microbes transform albumin into leucine, tyrosine, ammonium carbonate, fats into fatty acids and develop toxic-aromatic substances which, due to their stimulating power, appeal to degenerate tastes; in the same way as you can enjoy the salivating stimulus of the nicotine of tobacco.

All the products of the fermentation of cheese and which are the beginning of real putrefaction, are harmful and poisonous. It is easy to recognize unfermented cheeses first by their good smell, then by their light color, by the compact mass without veins or greenish grinds where real molds are collected with species of granules that are nothing more than worm eggs to be found in a second period of corruption.

Ricotta.

This other derivative of milk is also an extremely important food; it must be fresh, one or two days at the most and it is easy to recognize it because as soon as it is altered it immediately takes on an acrid odor and acid taste.

It contains all the substances of cheese, but with a much lower proportion of casein and therefore it is much easier to digest.

With it, infinite qualities of dishes and desserts are prepared, all very nutritious, light, and exquisite.

The oils and fats.

First of all, there is the pure olive oil of the highest quality, that is the one extracted from the mature olive harvested from the tree and which must therefore not exceed 2% acidity.

The olive oil that has fallen and dried on the ground, like that of the stone, must be discarded.

The first is a fat of the highest order due to its lightness and finesse given to it by the vegetable processing.

Besides having a very delicate fruit taste, it is very easy to be emulsified by the biliary juice and therefore easy to digest and completely assimilate; contains glycerin which makes it an excellent lubricant for the digestive tract.

Peanut, sesame, cotton, and other seed oils, when well refined, are also excellent fats for cooking, but it is advisable to combine them with olive oil or butter because, being neutral in taste, they need the sapidity that can be given to them by the latter.

Coconut fat is also excellent for cooking alone.

It is also edible raw mixed with the butter from which it takes the aroma.

All animal fats, due to their weight greater than that of vegetable fats and butter and the difficulty of being emulsified by bile, are difficult to digest, in addition to their more or less nauseating taste.

They contain some of the toxins of meat and are easy, due to the difficult digestive processing, to act directly on the proliferation of fat cells, thus promoting obesity.

Salads and vegetables.

Especially those that can be ingested raw are of great importance in the economy of our organism; in the raw state, they are very rich in vitamins and salts and are a vitalizing element par excellence and dissolving acids and toxins.

Cellulose, which is the main part of their construction, is necessary to constitute the mechanical mass that exerts pressure against the walls of the intestine, causing its peristaltic activity.

Thus the process of catabolism and the expulsion of digestive waste are favored, avoiding stagnation and the consequent absorption of toxins.

The danger of infectious diseases is a prejudice since when our organism is in conditions of attack, it will always and everywhere find enemies ready to attack it, whether it eats raw vegetables or not.

With the vegetable regime and healthy life, physically and ethically, the bacilli, which can be found both in raw vegetables and on any other food, on the edge of a glass where a fly has simply placed bread touched by infected fingers, will be attacked and destroyed by our natural defenses, which have not been exhausted and weakened by the laborious digestion of meat foods, which constitute a true environment of bacterial culture.

The salt

(chemically sodium chloride) is contained in our organism and it was therefore considered useful to supply it again in those small doses with which it is lost.

Exaggerating its use, it becomes irritating to the kidneys and mucous membranes of the intestine.

Celery salt is much more hygienic.

Aromas and spices.

In small and non-continuous doses, they are useful elements not only for the good taste of dishes but for the stimulation of gastric secretions and peristaltic movements.

By exaggerating their use, they are irritating, inflammatory and can produce serious disorders of the urinary and gastric tract.

Most harmful of all is black or white pepper, while cayenne and mustard are stronger but far less irritating. However, it is better to make as little use as possible.

The sugar.

This energetic element par excellence, concentrated in a very small volume, gives the greatest number of calories, absorbing itself very quickly without leaving any waste residue.

A small quantity of it ingested after a great effort is enough to immediately restore energy.

However, there is a big difference, to be taken into account, between inactive, neutralized sugar, in short, rendered inert by commercial manufacture and sugar supplied to us directly by nature through fruit, roots, milk, honey, etc.; this, inactive combination with mineral salts and diastases loaded with vitamins, is much more energetic, vitalizing and easier to be burned.

Fresh fruit and oily fruit.

Fresh fruit, and oily fruit (walnuts, almonds, hazelnuts, peanuts, pistachios, pine nuts, etc.), as we have already said, are in their entirety the complete and most rational food for man.

All nutritional elements are contained in their totality: proteins, carbon hydrates, fats, mineral salts, cellulose, vitamins, and biogenies.

Fresh fruits, with soft pulp, well ripe, are an ace, a true detoxifying and vitalizing food.

They are very suitable for feverish patients.

It is advisable to eat fruit with the peel when this is very thin and you are sure you can macerate it well with careful chewing.

Fruits are also very useful as repairers of the brain due to the considerable quantities of nitrogen and phosphoric acid they contain and are also precious for the dissolution of uric acids, due to the abundant potassium salts and organic acids they contain.

The vitamins.

This active principle, of supreme and necessary importance in the economy of our organism, was known by ancient Eastern wisdom under the Sanskrit generic term of Prana and experimental science, in its tireless investigative work to discern the truth from the imposture, into which ancient occult knowledge fell in the Middle Ages, has been able today experimentally ascertain the existence of this active principle in food and its indispensability in nutrition, because it is life.

Up to now, 5 classes of vitamins have been established, specifying them with the alphabetic letters A, B, C, D, E.

This denomination was given for the first time by Funk, in 1911 and the classifications by letters were given according to where they were extracted from and their specific characteristics.

Thus the vitamins isolated in the green part of vegetables, in milk, butter, and egg yolk were classified with the letter A.

They resist cooking and their lack of food causes developmental disorders, cachexia, rachitis.

Those with the letter B are found in the woody integument of cereals, in fresh and dried vegetables, also in milk, yeast, and bread; they resist the long boiling and their absence causes slimming, the beriberi of the Chinese (peeled rice eaters), and other serious disorders of the nervous system.

Those classified with the letter C are found in fresh vegetables, in fruit, also in milk, in whole eggs, and especially in citrus fruit juice.

They are sterilized by cooking.

Their absence generates scurvy, Barlow's disease, and other unspecified ailments.

While their absence causes such serious consequences, their presence stimulates nitrogen exchange and generates vital energies.

Vitamins D, are essential to avoid demineralization and therefore premonitory tuberculosis, chronic rheumatism, descaling menopause, etc.

Vitamins E, in abundance in wheat, lettuce, cabbage, etc., are very useful for growth and reproduction.

All other vital efficiencies not yet identified we will call them biogenic x.

Herbal teas.

They are divided into two categories: Infusions and decoctions.

For the former, lemon, tea, coffee, lime, chamomile, orange blossom, cedar, mandarin, lime, bitter orange, etc. are used.

They are prepared by pouring boiling water over the product from which the active yield is to be obtained.

Decoctions are formed with roots, vegetables, cocoa, lichens, quinine, pigeon, laurel, thyme, mallow, weed, wormwood, dried fruit, etc., whose values we will talk about later.

Raw infusions are also made in order not to kill the biogenic x

The drinks.

Excluding all those with alcoholic compounds, we can make them in large quantities with the sauce of all fruits starting with lemon, oranges, and other citrus fruits, which are all of a great value, and ending with the nutritious, milky ones extracted from sweet almonds, coconut, from barley, etc.

They are all useful both as dissolvents, in a healthy state of health, and as repairers in case of illness, when one cannot or must not eat.

Wine (it is the derivative of one of the best and most useful products of the vegetable kingdom which is grapes).

One of its components, sugar, is transformed into alcohol (due to the work of the bacteria called saccharomyces).

Our palate suggests and searches for a fine and very aged wine, which can be recognized by the delicious natural scent it emanates.

This comes from the fact that the alcohol in contact with the wine acids slowly transforms itself into ethers.

It is known how medicine uses commercial ethers (which is much less than the natural ethers of wine) to lift the organism and make it overcome the moment of crisis.

A few sips of excellent old wine, therefore, helps digestion and is an element of savings.

Vinegar.

Alcohol from wine to another bacteria, mycoderma-vinegar, is transformed into acetic acid.

It is deleterious and poisonous in our organism and its use must be forbidden except in cooking because, being the acetic acid volatilizable to boiling, put in

a small quantity in cooked dishes, it preserves only the aromatic part, which is not harmful.

In salads, it is, therefore, preferable to use lemon, which instead gives them the freshness of taste and vitalizing energies.

Some diets

These diets are recommendations, so you should consult your doctor before starting the diet

Diet for the obese

Obesity is an imbalance of exchange due in large part to proper or atavic dietary errors for which it is by modifying the causes that the best results are obtained.

The obese must certainly resort to the following raw naturism:

The organism rationally and without problems

The patient must strictly adhere to the following treatment if he really wants to put his organism ruined by obesity in order.

With this diet, which is the synthesis of years of study, he will have surprising results and without any suffering, he will decrease in 18 days of treatment, from 11 to 33 lb.

The sense of well-being, lightness, agility, and good humor immediately comes from it.

Leading precisely to a true renewal and rejuvenation of the whole being.

First day

Morning: 1/2 grapefruit or an orange or 1 lemon sliced with honey, an egg (Possibly raw with lemon juice, salt, and mustard if you like, or boiled to the point you want), a slice of toast, ½ lettuce, tea, coffee without sugar or milk.

Evening: Unfermented cheese 2,5 oz., 6 slices watermelon, ½ grapefruit, or orange or 1 lemon sliced with honey, tea, or coffee.

Second day

Morning: Two oranges or 2,20 lb. of watermelon, 1 egg, a slice of toast, 2 lettuce, tea, or coffee.

Evening: 2 eggs, a lettuce heart or 4 roots, a tomato or an apple, an orange or ½ grapefruit, tea or coffee without sugar or milk.

Third day

Morning: 2 grapefruit or an orange or 2,20 lb. of watermelon, one egg, 4 raw artichoke hearts, or 8 slices of watermelon, tea, or coffee.

Evening: Fresh cheese 2,5 oz., an egg, 3 radishes, or a cabbage 4 olives, tea, or coffee without sugar or milk.

Fourth day

Morning: 2 eggs, a slice of toast, a tomato or an apple, or 2 raw artichokes, ½ grapefruit or an orange, tea or coffee.

Evening: 8.50 fl. oz. (US) of whole milk, 4 sugar-free biscuits, an orange or 2 grapefruit, tea or coffee without sugar or milk.

Fifth day

Morning: An orange or 2,20 lb. of watermelon, one egg, 4 olives, tea or coffee.

Evening: Fresh cheese, a slice of toast, 8 slices of cocoa or 2 apples, an orange, tea or coffee without sugar or milk.

Sixth day

Morning: Fresh cheese, 2 tomatoes or 2 artichokes or 4 raw roots, 2 melons or watermelon or 2 oranges, tea or coffee.

Evening: one egg, 3 radishes, 2 tomatoes or 2 sour apples, 6 slices of watermelon or 2 hearts of lettuce, tea or coffee without sugar or milk.

Seventh day

Morning: 2 eggs, a tomato or a sour apple, a slice of toast, ½ melon or 2 pears, tea or coffee.

Evening: An orange, fresh cheese, honey with 2 biscuits, a raw pepper or 2 raw artichokes or 2 lettuce hearts, tea or coffee without sugar or milk.

Eighth day

Morning: An egg, 4 olives, 10 slices of watermelon or 2 sour apples, 2 grapefruit or an orange, tea or coffee without sugar or milk.

Evening: Fresh cheese, a slice of toast, a tomato or an apple, 2 oranges, tea, or coffee without sugar or milk.

Ninth day

<u>Morning</u>: 12 well-chewed raw almonds or hazelnuts, a pepper or 3 raw artichokes or two cabbage, 6 slices of watermelon or 2 sour apples, an orange or ½ grapefruit, tea or coffee without sugar or milk.

<u>Evening</u>: An egg, tomato, or an apple, 3 roots, lemon with honey, ½ melon or watermelon or two oranges, tea or coffee without sugar or milk.

Day 10

<u>Morning</u>: 2 eggs, a slice of toast, 6 olives, an orange or 2 melons, tea or coffee.

<u>Evening</u>: Cheese, 6 slices of watermelon or 2 sour apples, grapefruit or 2 oranges or 2,20 lb. melon, tea or coffee without sugar or milk.

Eleventh day

<u>Morning</u>: An egg, 2 breadsticks, 2 tomatoes or a pear, ½ melon or an orange, tea or coffee without sugar or milk.

<u>Evening</u>: Fresh cheese, a heart of lettuce or raw do pepper, 6 slices of watermelon or 2 sour apples, tea or coffee without sugar and milk.

Twelfth day

<u>Morning</u>: 2 eggs, tomato or an apple, a slice of toast or 2 breadsticks, a grapefruit or 2 oranges or 2,20 lb. of melon, tea or coffee without sugar or milk.

Evening: A cup of 4 milk, 6 slices of watermelon or 4 raw roots, an orange or half a melon, tea or coffee without sugar or milk.

Thirteenth day

Morning: Fresh cheese, raw lettuce or pepper, tomato or an apple, an orange or 2 melon, tea or coffee.

Evening: 2 eggs, a slice of toast, 2 tomatoes, or an apple. an orange or 2 grapefruit or 2,20 lb. of watermelon, tea, or coffee without sugar or milk.

Fourteenth day

Morning: An egg, 6 slices of watermelon or 2 raw artichokes or a pepper, an orange or 2 melons, tea or coffee without sugar or milk.

Evening: 12 raw almonds or hazelnuts, 2 pears, an orange or 2 grapefruit, or 2,20 lb. of melon, tea, or coffee without sugar or milk

Fifteenth day

Morning: 2 eggs, tomato or an apple, 6 slices of watermelon or 2 raw cabbage, an orange or 2 melons, coffee or tea without sugar or milk.

Evening: Fresh cheese, tomato or 3 radishes, 8 almonds or raw hazelnuts, an orange or 2 melon, tea or coffee without sugar or milk.

For the 16th, 17th and 18th day repeat the first three

Depending on the results, the aforementioned regime can be repeated two or three times a year with no danger or minimal damage to the subject.

It is preferable to do it in the summer because with it you no longer suffer from the heat.

It is useful to occasionally take a few teaspoons of heavy magnesia.

Eggs are preferable raw, but never cooked with fat.

Diet for the gouty

Do not use industrial sugar.

Excellent purées and soups without aromas of spices.

Milk is good to stretch it a little water.

Raw naturism, heals completely if done on time.

Diet, for those suffering from eczema

Eczema is generally caused by unsuitable nutrition, meat foods, and fish, in particular, dried Scarlet legumes, while green ones and raw vegetables are very good.

Of the cereals exclude oats.

Ban coffee, and take tea very lightly.

No complicated sauces, cheeses, sweets, pastries, fresh bread, canned foods, or sterile in any way.

Going on a raw naturist diet is the best remedy.

Diabetic diet

Good eggs. Exclude starch and replace them with many vegetable fats and cream to obtain the calories of the former.

Many vegetables, preferably raw.

The crushed almonds and oilseeds, put in dishes, both soup and salted, etc., are excellent for replacing cereals and legumes.

Gluten-free bread and pasta; and when it is tolerated, take also rye bread or even almond flour and plasmon.

Zucchini and the whole raw cabbage family are recommended, especially if served plain and seasoned with oil and lemon.

Good chocolate made with sugar-cocoa.

Vermifuge diet

First of all purge with a vegetable purgative, and then every morning, fasting, for four days, give half a tablespoon of the following decoction: 2 oz. of Santolina herbs boiled in three cups of water and collected in two thirds.

The food will be made from toast rubbed with a little garlic and soaked in lemon juice, oil, salt, and parsley, a little green legume puree, fresh fruit, and well-ground oily fruit.

Double portion for adults.

Diet for the old men

All vegetarian eating is excellent, especially raw (see Appendix), as long as you choose things not to chew too much, avoiding irritants: pepper, mustards, cayenne, spices and aromas, substances with cooked acids, condiments, and complicated sauces.

Limit starchy, possibly toasted bread and never fresh bread, better raw bread. Mashed cereal flours and green legumes are excellent, as well as ripe fruit with soft pulp, oily ones must be pounded and eaten immediately.

Avoid fried vegetables and well-cooked dried legumes.

Pastry shops, sweets, and over-rich puddings should be limited. Light tea and cocoa are excellent drinks.

Diet to gain weight

To all dishes rich in starchy or fat add plenty of sweet fruit.

Go to bed early and get up early with a good breakfast with butter, honey, and abundant fresh fruit.

Diet for constipated

Naturism is the best regime, but if you want to limit yourself to vegetarianism, just add a plate of prunes, both fresh and dried, waxed in water, to your common meals, adjusting the quantity with your experience according to the grade of constipation from which one suffers and of individual tolerance.

Raw almonds are also excellent and all cucurbits, possibly raw, are indicated.

Diet for stomach sufferers

The raw food regime, if done with perseverance and discernment, completely puts in order the organism sacrificed by our personal and atavistic errors.

It is not possible to give precise data valid for all people, since each organism has particular tolerances and idiosyncrasies.

The interesting thing is to abolish cooking. Through cooking, in addition to killing most of the vitamins and all of the biogeny x, chemical combinations still well-known occur, which alter and create harmful sub-products.

Let's see for example the tomato, which while raw is an excellent dissolving, vitalizing, and highly digestible vegetable. cooked it produces uric acids, dyspepsia, liver stones, etc.

So go on a raw regime by choosing and distributing food with your own experience.

Even sick with some gastric diseases considered incurable up to now, they recover completely with the raw food diet.

Rational way of distributing meals

Known which are the elements necessary for our nutrition, namely: carbohydrates, proteins (egg whites), mineral salts, fats, cellulose, vitamins, and biogenesis x, and we know that we have them all in the natural products, now let's see how to distribute them harmoniously throughout the day.

In the morning it is useful to take something that prepares us well for the hard work, both manual and mental; and for this purpose, a light revitalizing and dynamogenic meal with nutrient substances of a little volume and which do not require excessive digestive work is indicated. It can be excellently made up of some raw fruit or vegetables: tomato, watermelon, melon, or seed fruit such as almonds, walnuts, hazelnuts, etc. to give the energetic-vitalizing action.

You can add some light protein food with milk, bread and butter, jams and honey, and some stimulants such as coffee, tea, or cocoa, lightly and in small doses.

At noon, when we need to repair the exhausted organism with work, a complete diet is necessary, which can consist of the first course of soup, or dry pasta or timbale, to supply ourselves mainly with carbon hydrates and then a partition to draw on the mineral salts, the cellulose, and the fat.

A few more proteins, besides that part we took in the first one, can be ingested with a main dish or with eggs, cheese or dessert.

It is good to remember that our organism does not need more than 30 oz. 1,8of protein per day and more is harmful.

With fruit we complete the meal by drawing a large part of it vitalizing, sugar in its best form, cellulose, dissolving acids, etc.

Around 5 am, especially for those who work very mentally, a cup of tea or light coke is a refreshment.

The raw food in the evening enough to refresh oneself without loading the stomach, it being very hygienic to go to bed to let the body rest as completely as possible and that is without giving it the task of laborious digestion.

A puree, some vegetables or salad, and a few plates of light sauce would be enough pastry, without ever omitting fruit.

All raw food is even better.

For those who love a more thrifty diet either for economic reasons, or because they are more attracted to mental or spiritual life, already knowing that it is very sufficient to fully nourish themselves (and certainly more hygienically than with cooked foods) a piece of black bread is enough, a raw egg

or some fresh milk, and assorted fruit with oil seeds (walnuts, almonds, peanuts, hazelnuts, etc.).

It is also possible to combine modest and complete meals as follows: in the morning bread and fruit or green vegetables (cucumber, tomato, onion, melon, etc.), or a bowl of fresh milk; at noon a soup or a raw egg, a salad or a raw vegetable and mixed fruit; in the evening a slice of raw cheese and fruit.

In all ways, it is always good to vary because the repetition of food tires us.

The multiplicity of differences make the complete and in the alternatives, the organism finds rest and the choice of various small elements.

It is also good to follow what the seasons provide us in more abundance and inexpensively because this too has reason to be.

Let's see, for example, how acidic and juicy fruit abounds in the strong summer heat which refreshes us, and supplies us with replacement fluids, while in winter oilseeds and dried fruit give us calories and more energetic nourishment.

Cookbook

The doses of each formula are generally for six people

Almond eggs

Take a cup of breadcrumbs and a cup of boiling milk and let it soak.

Add 6 beaten eggs, salt, pepper and half a cup of peeled and pounded walnuts and almonds.

Put in molds and cook in a double boiler.

Eggs to the empress

Boil the eggs hard-boiled, peel them, and cut them in half, removing the yolks.

Make a pesto with an onion, a clove of garlic, a bunch of parsley, a bunch of mints, salt, and pepper, sprinkling with vinegar.

Mix with the egg yolks and pass through a sieve.

Fill all the whites and cover them with a good mayonnaise sauce by sowing chopped capers and gherkins in vinegar on them.

Garnish with salad or boiled potatoes.

Eggs in fricassee

Cook them broken in water, place them each on a slice of fried bread and pour a fricassee sauce on the plate. Make the fricassee sauce with this method:

Brown a tablespoon of flour in a knob of butter on the stove.

Gradually pour in 8,50 fl. oz. of water seasoned with salt, pepper and chopped parsley.

Boil a little, get off the heat and pour in 2 tablespoons of cream or fresh butter and 2 egg yolks, mixing well and binding.

Squeeze half a lemon and serve.

Sage eggs

Make a pesto with:

1,8 oz. of capers, 3 sage leaves, 8 cloves of garlic boiled for 10 minutes and 2,30 oz. of bread marrow soaked in vinegar or lemon sauce seasoning with salt and pepper.

Switch to the sieve.

Put this sauce in the bottom of the dish and arrange 8 hard eggs cut to taste and sprinkle over sage and other herbs.

Terrine of truffled eggs

Shred 6 hard-boiled eggs and divide them into the terrines.

Cut into cubes 7 oz. of mozzarella cheese or other fresh unfermented cheese and divide it also above, cover with a béchamel.

Make the béchamel with this method:

Melt a piece of butter with a spoonful of flour, salt, and white pepper.

Gradually add 135 fl. oz. of milk and cook, stirring constantly.

Sow chopped truffles, place a small piece of butter for each bowl, and bake.

Eggs stuffed with chicken (Pseudo)

Make 6 hard-boiled eggs, cut them in half, remove the yolks that you will mix well with the pseudo chicken filling.

Make the pseudo chicken fill with this method:

Milk 66 fl. oz., butter 3,5 oz., 4 tablespoons flour, 3 eggplants, 8 walnuts, 3 egg yolks, onion.

Melt the butter with the flour and a pinch of salt and, always stirring, gradually add the milk, a very small spoonful of onion, parsley.

Then, fill the half eggs rounding them so that they look like whole eggs.

Flour them, pass them to beaten egg, then to breadcrumbs, and fry them.

shredded and pepper.

As soon as it is well blended, go down.

Fry the peeled and diced aubergines, then pour them into the sauce together with the pounded walnuts and mix them with the yolks.

To make it even more delicious, you can add chopped truffles and 1,8 oz.of grated parmesan cheese.

These ingredients must be kept ready before cooking the milk.

Eggs or pseudo-newborn eggs

Take the yolks of well-boiled eggs and pass them through a sieve.

Mix the puree with as much raw egg white as you need to handle them and make small balls of different sizes like newborn eggs.

Throw them in slowly boiling water and sortie them as soon as they are firm.

The new means, use them as follows.

Stuffed eggs without yolks

To use the hard-boiled egg whites, from which you have removed the yolks to make another dish, fill them with a filling to your taste,

preferably the chicken one, pass them in flour, then in beaten egg, bread them and fry them with a side dish of wafer potatoes.

Eggs marinara or in green sauce

Pound the mint and parsley with a piece of bread marinade in vinegar or lemon, and pass it through a sieve seasoning with oil, salt and pepper.

Cook the hard eggs, peel them, cut them in half and remove the yolks without breaking the white.

Crush them and mix them with part of the aforementioned sauce, adding pepper and salt, and if you like, a little finely chopped garlic.

Fill the egg halves, arrange them on a plate, and pour the rest of the sauce over them.

Eggs to the monk

Boil 6 eggs, and when they are hard, peel them and cut them in half.

Remove the yolks and mix them with the same weight of ricotta, 5 oz.of grated parmesan, 8 walnuts, salt, pepper, and chopped parsley.

Fill the egg halves, flour them, pass them into the egg, then into breadcrumbs and fry them.

Eggs with herbs

Put parsley and chopped onion, salt, pepper, half a glass of white wine, half a spoonful of butter dusted with flour in a saucepan, and boil for a quarter of an hour with chopped herbs.

When the sauce is well tied, put in a dish some eggs cooked with this method:

Put a saucepan three-quarters full of water on the heat, two tablespoons of vinegar (when the acetic acid boils it evaporates), and a little salt; when the water is boiling, the eggs are broken little by little.

When cooked to the desired point, they rise with the skimmer to arrange them in a salty dish with any hot sauce.

Pour the sauce over and sprinkle with breadcrumbs and toasted in a pan with butter.

Scrambled eggs

Put the eggs in a saucepan with a piece of butter and cook slowly, stirring constantly.

You can add a few tablespoons of mozzarella, chopped herbs or grated parmesan.

Get off as soon as you coagulate.

Scrambled eggs with pik-pacchio

Take a "pik-pacchio" sauce that you can make like this:

Cut 2 large onions into long and thin fillets and fry them in 5 or 6 tablespoons of excellent olive oil;

just lightly browned throw in 4,40 lb. of very ripe tomato from which you have carefully removed all the peel with all the seeds and cut into small pieces;

add salt, pepper, 1 clove of garlic, a pinch of saffron, finely chopped parsley, and basil, and cook until you have a very thick sauce.

Then mix it with raw eggs and a piece of butter, salt, and pepper.

Put on the fire without leaving to stir until they tie at the desired point.

Serve with fried croutons.

Eggs with French peas

Cook some green peas by throwing them in boiling water and salt, and put them to dry.

Arrange the fried croutons in a refractory dish, sprinkle the beaten eggs on top and mix with the peas.

Place on the embers and put on fire or cook until they coagulate.

Aurora eggs

Cut the hard-boiled eggs in half, remove the yolks that you put in a bowl with a piece of butter, chopped herbs, salt, a little grated nutmeg, a little bread soaked in milk, and squeeze; mix everything.

Fill the white halves, arrange them in a buttered refractory dish and pour a layer of béchamel over them.

Make the béchamel with this method:

Melt a piece of butter with a spoonful of flour, salt, and white pepper.

Gradually add 135 fl. oz. of milk and cook, stirring constantly.

Bake with butter on top.

Eggs in terrines

For each one egg, take a bowl, put a small piece of liquid butter and chopped herbs, break the egg, cover with grated parmesan cheese, and bake until cooked, serving in the same bowls.

Mirror eggs with asparagus

Cut the asparagus into small pieces, taking only the tender;

blanch them in boiling water, put them in a saucepan with a piece of butter, parsley and chopped onion, place them on the fire, sow a pinch of flour and moisten with a little water.

Cook sprinkling with a little salt, place on the refractory plate, break the eggs on top, season with a little salt, pepper and nutmeg; cook on the grill and with a lid on fire.

Serve very hot.

Salsite eggs

Boil some water in a saucepan, and when boiling, add the number of eggs you want, let it boil for 5 minutes, and then immediately put them in freshwater.

Carefully remove the peel, so that the white does not break.

In this way, you will be able to have semi-hard eggs that are flexible to your fingers.

You will serve them whole with white sauce or green sauce, skip tartar, spicy sauce, or whatever else you like best.

Eggs with Indian béchamel

Cut the hard eggs into wheels and mix them with the béchamel sauce.

Make the béchamel with this method:

Melt a piece of butter with a spoonful of flour, salt, and white pepper. Gradually add 135 fl. oz. of milk and cook, stirring constantly.

to which you have added a teaspoon of curry.

Make curry with this method:

powder to flavor soups, sauces, soups, etc. It is already prepared in the original English brand saucepans.

It can be easily prepared at home by mixing three-fifths of sweet red pepper, one-fifth of hot peppers (cayenne pepper), and one-fifth of saffron, all well dried and ground. The dose of the cayenne can vary according to its spicy strength and so that of the saffron.

Sprinkle with butter, cumin, and bake.

Bagged eggs

Put a saucepan three-quarters full of water on the heat, two tablespoons of vinegar (when the acetic acid boils it evaporates), and a little salt; when the water is boiling, the eggs are broken little by little.

When cooked to the desired point, they rise with the skimmer to arrange them in a salty dish with any hot sauce.

Florentine-style eggs

Cut 9 hard eggs in half, remove the yolks and peel them with 3,5 oz.of butter,5,30 oz. of fresh ricotta and 3,5 oz. of grated parmesan, a little salt and pepper.

Put in a saucepan by adding 4 raw egg yolks and an egg white until stiff.

Stir and put on a light heat, continuing to stir until it tightens.

Fill the hard white halves of it, and the one over it you will lay in a layer on a refractory plate, placing the filled halves on top.

Drizzle with the béchamel.

Make the béchamel with this method:

Melt a piece of butter with a spoonful of flour, salt and white pepper.

Gradually add 135 fl. oz. of milk and cook, stirring constantly.

Then, sprinkle with parmesan and drizzle with the butter.

Reheat in the oven and serve.

Eggs in black butter

Break the eggs into a refractory dish.

Cook them, and approach them without touching a red-hot scoop to cook the yellows.

Serve by pouring over a black butter sauce.

Make the butter sauce with this method:

Put the butter in a pan and let it brown without burning it.

Put some parsley in this moment, making it fry, and then pour it on the dish.

In the pan itself, heat up a little vinegar which you will also pour over the food.

Eggs in a carriage

Fry them one by one and place each one on a toast of fried bread.

Fry slices of fresh cheese, placing one on each egg, and pour plenty of tomato sauce over them.

Stewed eggs

Cut into hard halves.

Prepare part of the chopped onion roasted in oil and then sprinkle with water where you have melted the saffron in hot, put the half eggs in them sprinkling them with chopped parsley, salt, and pepper, cover, and cook until all become yellow for the color of saffron.

Serve with a side of fried croutons.

Egg timbale

Whisk 8 egg whites until stiff and mix in 66 fl. oz. of béchamel.

Make the béchamel with this method:

Melt a piece of butter with a spoonful of flour, salt and white pepper.

Gradually add 135 fl. oz. of milk and cook, stirring constantly.

7 oz.of grated parmesan cheese, 10 plague walnuts, abundant chopped parsley and egg yolks.

Pour without delay into a mold greased with butter and sprinkled with breadcrumbs.

Place in the oven and turn over on a plate with a towel.

Eggs in shell

Cut 4 hard eggs into small pieces and mix them with an equal quantity of mushroom filling.

Make the filling of mushroom with this method:

40 fl. oz. of mozzarella and cayenne pepper.

Put them in the shells, let a little melted butter drip, and bake.

Then, roasted 2 onions well shredded in butter and just golden, throw in 0,70 oz.of dried mushrooms were cured in water for an hour and shredded and 12 walnuts pounded, adding two bay leaves, nutmeg, pepper, parsley, and salt.

Cook a little and drop.

Apart from soaking 3,5 oz.of bread marrow in milk and put it on the fire, stirring until a batter is formed in which you will pour the first seasoning cold.

Remove the bay leaves and add 4 egg yolks.

Mix vigorously.

Use it for fillings.

Fried egg chops

Make the benches as with this method, but small ones:

Half 33 fl. oz. of milk, 2 eggs, flour 7 oz., jam.

Melt the flour with the milk starting little by little so that there are no lumps and then mix the eggs that you have first beaten well.

Put a piece of butter as much as a walnut in the pan and when it is melted pour in a small cup of the liquid.

Once cooked on one side, turn over using a plate.

With a dexterity that can only be achieved with a long habit, they can be turned, pushing into the pan on the top

giving a push in the direction of rotation towards you.

Place the fried disc on a plate and wrap the jam inside.

Sprinkle some sugar with a hot scoop, touch it so that it caramelizes.

They can be filled as desired with marzipan, cassata cream, white wine, etc.

Then put them on the table and fill them with a topping of bread soaked in milk and grated parmesan cheese, mix with a little onion browning, chopped parsley, salt, and pepper.

Make the chops by turning them over, insert them on the skewers alternating them with slices of bread, plaster them with bechamel, flour them, pass them into the egg, then into breadcrumbs and fry them.

Pizza eggs

Put some oil in a baking tray or refractory plate and break the eggs.

Cover them with thin slices of fresh cheese, add some peeled half tomatoes, sprinkle with salt, pepper, oregano and minced garlic and bake.

Eggs with salad lettuce

Cut hard eggs and very fine lettuce into wedges.

Dissolve some of the yolks in vinegar and mustard, then mix in the oil, season with salt and pepper and pour over the lettuce with the eggs.

Poached eggs

Cook the broken eggs in water with this method:

Put a saucepan three-quarters full of water on the heat, two tablespoons of vinegar (when the acetic acid boils it evaporates), and a little salt; when the water is boiling, the eggs are broken little by little.

When cooked to the desired point, they rise with the skimmer to arrange them in a salty dish with any hot sauce.

Then let them cool on the napkin.

Cut very fine slices of fresh cheese and after dipping them for a moment in boiling water wrap the eggs.

Flour them, pass them to beaten egg, then to breadcrumbs, and fry them in abundant oil.

Vegetable-style eggs

Take large tomatoes that can contain one egg for each, also empty the seeds, sprinkle with a salt, place on the refractory plate, and break an egg for each tomato.

Put a slice of fresh cheese, some butter, and bake.

Clouded eggs

Beat the whites until stiff and then add some chopped onion and parsley, salt and pepper.

Pour into a refractory dish with butter, pour half a glass of mozzarella into the center and place all the whole egg yolks on top of it at an equal distance.

Cook in a light oven and serve immediately.

Omelette with herbs

Break the eggs into a bowl adding salt, pepper, finely chopped herbs, beat everything well, melt some butter in a pan and toss in the beaten.

When it takes color, fold on itself and serve immediately.

Eggs with mushrooms

Take 12 hard eggs and remove the whole yolk.

Put some chopped mushrooms in a saucepan that you will cook with butter, salt and pepper and add,

when cooked, shredded hard egg whites.

Put everything on the plate, garnishing with fried croutons and placing the whole hard egg yolks on top.

Chilean-style eggs

Make the Chilean-style aubergines with this method:

Cut the aubergines in two and boil them in water and salt.

Let it cool and scoop out the pulp with a spoon, leaving the outside healthy like a wand.

Chop these pulps well and mix them with peeled tomato, grated parmesan, chopped parsley, breadcrumbs, salt, cayenne pepper and fill the shells.

Arrange in a pan, put some small pieces of butter, and bake.

Then on top of each place an eye-fried egg and ketchup sauce.

You can make the ketchup with this method:

Pass 2,20 lb. tomato and cook with 1 oz.of sugar, 8 fl. oz.. of vinegar, 0,1 oz.of cinnamon powder, 0,1 oz.of cloves in powder, 0,1 oz. of ground chamomile and a pinch of cayenne.

Make it tighten well and keep in the bottle after having melted 0,1 oz. of salicylic acid.

Egg anemole

Beat 6 eggs and make some open omelets turned over with a plate.

Make a paste of ricotta and grated parmesan, salt, and pepper, which you will put on each disc, wrapping it like a chop.

Arrange them in a refractory dish or baking tray, sprinkle with parmesan cheese, sauce with velvety, and let them encrust in the oven.

Eggs Sultana

Make a baked bread of bread and milk.

When tight, go down and add 4,4 oz. of grated parmesan.

Whisk 5 egg whites until stiff and mix with the breadcrumbs together with the yolks.

Take a saucepan that can contain three-quarters of the above composition, add two glasses of broth and boil them.

At this moment pour this composition without ever mixing or touching it, as it must come out whole.

Turn on itself only with the handle of the saucepan, and when it is firm, let it cool a little, and then, putting the lid on, let the broth strain and turn into a plate.

Tie the broth and pour it over.

Lumberjack eggs

Put a quarter of 34 fl. oz. of red wine and 8,50 fl. oz. of broth in a saucepan, or in the absence perhaps water; add a bunch of herbs, 1 onion, 1 clove of garlic, salt, pepper, and a little spice;

boil for 10 minutes, put on the side on the stove, but so that it continues to boil and break 6 fresh eggs one by one, removing them with a slotted spoon until they are fried.

Let the sauce reduce, tying with 1,8 oz.of butter and a tablespoon of flour, pour this sauce over the eggs and serve.

Eggs with subisso

Make an egg omelet that you will cut into strips in the guise of cutters.

Arrange them on a hot plate and pour over a subisso sauce, heating slightly.

Make subisso sauce with this method:

Three onions, 1,8 oz.of butter, 4 fl. oz. of mozzarella, 25 fl. oz. of milk, 1 oz.of flour, salt, and white pepper.

Slice the onions, boil them slowly in a little water and when well cooked, pass them through a sieve, melt the butter with the flour on the stove, add the salt, pepper and pour in the milk little by little.

Stir until it boils.

Go down and add the pureed onions and mozzarella.

Eggs with pumpkin

Eggs 6, parmesan cheese 3,5 oz., pumpkin lb. 1, butter 2,65 oz., almonds 3,5 oz.

Choose that tender pumpkin that comes apart during cooking and cut it into small pieces.

Cook it with water and salt and pass it through a sieve.

Just lukewarm, mix 1, 8 oz.of butter, the peeled and chopped almonds and the cheese together with the already beaten eggs, with a little salt.

Pour the liquid into a refractory dish, sprinkle over the rest of the cheese, a little breadcrumbs, small pieces of butter and bake.

Spinach eggs

8 eggs, 66 fl. oz. milk, butter 2,65 oz., spinach lb. 1.

Boil the spinach in water and salt, drain and pass them through a sieve, dissolve 1,8 oz.of the butter with a spoon full of flour and slowly mix the milk and finally the pureed spinach.

Pour over the stuffed eggs, make with this method:

Put a saucepan three-quarters full of water on the heat, two tablespoons of vinegar (when the acetic acid boils it evaporates) and a little salt; when the water is boiling, the eggs are broken little by little.

When cooked to the desired point, they rise with the skimmer to arrange them in a salty dish with any hot sauce.

Truffled eggs

8 eggs, 17 fl. oz. milk, parmesan 3,5 oz., truffles 3,5 oz., butter 2,65 oz.

Make a béchamel with this method: melt a piece of butter with a spoonful of flour, salt, and white pepper.

Gradually add 135 fl. oz. of milk and cook, stirring constantly.

Then add the chopped truffles.

Let it cool and mix in the beaten eggs and parmesan.

Pour into a baking pan or refractory plate, sprinkle with breadcrumbs, drop some butter, and bake.

Pink eggs

Do as above, but instead of bechamel with truffles, use tomato sauce.

Egg medallions in fricassee

Bread marinade 7 oz., eggs 10, butter 3,5 oz., parmesan 3,5 oz.; 2 lemons, 7 fl. oz. milk.

Soak the bread in milk and whisk all the egg whites with a pinch of salt.

Mix them with the bread, adding seven of the egg yolks and the grated parmesan.

Melt some butter in the pan and throw in half of the mixture.

When cooked, turn over and make the second. Melt the 3 egg yolks separately

left, with the lemon juice, a glass (4 fl. oz.) of water and abundant chopped parsley, adding 2 tablespoons of flour, salt and pepper.

Let it coagulate on the fire and pour over the medallions.

Homemade eggs

Break the eggs into a refractory dish, cover with slices of fresh cheese, pour some bechamel, butter and bake.

Make Béchamel sauce with this method:

Melt a piece of butter with a spoonful of flour, salt and white pepper.

Gradually add 135 fl. oz. of milk and cook, stirring constantly.

Eggs with green sauce

Make the hard-boiled eggs, cut them in half, arrange them on a plate, and pour over the Florentine green sauce.

Make the Florentine green sauce with this method:

Finely chop some capers, a small onion, and a clove of garlic, mash everything with a knife, and place in a gravy boat.

Add some chopped parsley, basil, and a little shredded sage, and dissolve everything with two-thirds of fine oil and one-third of lemon juice.

Then, the yolks must be mixed with a little of the same sauce and put back into the hard whites before adding them.

Concealed eggs

Prepare a ravioli pasta, spread it out to a thickness of 2-3 mm. about;

separately you will have made a béchamel with this method with double the flour and add some grated parmesan:

Melt a piece of butter with a spoonful of flour, salt and white pepper.

Gradually add 135 fl. oz. of milk and cook, stirring constantly.

Put half a spoonful of this mixture on the pasta leaf, on top a half hard egg, cover again with a little more of the mixture, fold over the leaf, cut with a wheel and fry in oil.

Put 1,8 oz.of butter and a spoonful of flour.

Cook slowly adding 135 fl. oz. of milk.

Finally, descend and add 4 fl. oz. of mozzarella, pepper and salt.

Simple omelette

Break the eggs into a bowl adding salt, pepper, beat everything well, melt some butter in a pan and toss in the beaten.

When it takes color, fold on itself and serve immediately.

Omelette with cheese

Break the eggs into a bowl adding salt, pepper, finely chopped herbs, beat everything well, melt some butter in a pan and toss in the beaten.

When it takes color, fold on itself and serve immediately.

stirring before cooking some good grated parmesan.

Mushroom omelette

Break the eggs into a bowl adding salt, pepper, finely chopped herbs, beat everything well, melt some butter in a pan and toss in the beaten.

When it takes color, fold on itself and serve immediately.

Adding some mushrooms cut into strips, and cooked in butter.

Omelette with truffles

Break the eggs into a bowl adding salt, pepper, finely chopped herbs, beat everything well, melt some butter in a pan and toss in the beaten.

When it takes color, fold on itself and serve immediately.

Adding truffles cut into small pieces.

Omelette with asparagus

Break the eggs into a bowl adding salt, pepper, finely chopped herbs, beat everything well, melt some butter in a pan and toss in the beaten. When it takes color, fold on itself and serve immediately.

Before turning, throw in some tender boiled asparagus.

Sicilian omelette

Whip the whites of 10 eggs; grated 3,5 oz.of bread and the same amount of parmesan, finely chopped parsley, and onion mix everything including the yolks thrown in a pan with oil; man color continuously turns on itself forming a roll.

Serve whole with a side of fried potatoes.

Omelette with tomato

Do as above, cut into slices and arrange on a hot plate pouring a tomato sauce.

Make tomato sauce with this method:

Take the ripe tomato, wash it and mash it in a saucepan; add 2 chopped onions for each lb., 1 clove of garlic, and some basil leaves.

After about 3/4 hours of cooking, pass it and put it back on the heat condensing it with salt, pepper and butter, and oil in equal parts.

Make it tighten to the point you need. If the tomato is very acidic, add a pinch of bicarbonate and a little sugar.

Omelette with spinach

Make a simple omelet with this method:

Break the eggs into a bowl adding salt, pepper, finely chopped herbs, beat everything well, melt some butter in a pan and toss in the beaten.

When it takes color, fold on itself and serve immediately.

Then, adding some boiled, chopped, and sautéed spinach in butter before turning.

Onion omelette

Cut a nice onion into fillets; let it come to moderate heat with a little butter; remove from the heat as soon as it is cooked without being roasted and add 6 beaten eggs: add salt, pepper, and chopped parsley, and fry.

Omelette with walnuts

Break the eggs into a bowl adding salt, pepper, finely chopped herbs, beat everything well, melt some butter in a pan and toss in the beaten.

When it takes color, fold on itself and serve immediately.

Adding a pounded walnut for each egg.

Macaroni omelette

Mix the previously cooked macaroni cut into small pieces with the beaten eggs, as well as plenty of grated parmesan cheese and fry leaving it like focaccia.

Omelette with bread or ricotta

Fry a few slices of bread, first remove the crust and dip them in the egg then in the flour and finally in the breadcrumbs.

Then you will put on the omelette just thrown into the pan and turn them so that the bread stays inside.

You can also put some ricotta.

Castellana fondue

Put 3,5 oz.of butter to melt, add 1,4 oz.of flour, 4 egg yolks, and half a glass of milk.

Boil for 2 minutes, working continuously. Remove from the heat, mix immediately with 3,5 oz.of parmesan, 3,5oz. gruyere cheese, salt, pepper, nutmeg, and 2 egg whites beaten until stiff.

Fill them with paper boxes or refractory terrines to two-thirds and cook in the oven.

Town fondue

Put 6 egg yolks, 0,70 oz.of flour that is well dry and 0,4 oz.of potato starch; mix everything, pour a glass of double mozzarella, and 1,8 oz.of fresh butter in small pieces.

Put on the heat and cook for 3 minutes, taking care to constantly turn.

Remove from the fire, mix 7 oz.of grated parmesan cheese, 5,30 oz.gruyere cheese and diced truffles.

Add salt, pepper, a very little nutmeg, and 2 whipped egg whites; fill the terrines to two-thirds and cook in a moderate oven.

Puffed omelette

It is necessary to make and serve it portion by portion.

Beat the whites until stiff with a pinch of salt and take a portion in a bowl, quickly mix egg yolk and toss in the pan where a piece of butter is frying; put together and turn over continuously

with the pallet without letting it take color until you have made a well-swollen bale to be served immediately because when it cools it deflates.

Omelette flag

Make 3 simple omelets with this method:

break the eggs into a bowl adding salt, pepper, finely chopped herbs, beat everything well, melt some butter in a pan and toss in the beaten.

When it takes color, fold on itself and serve immediately.

Then, in which you will have mixed cooked and sieved spinach in one, tomato in the other, the third you will make only whites while the reds you will mix in the tomato one.

Arrange flat so that the white comes in the middle.

Olivetan pseudo-tripe omelette

Make simple omelets with this method:

Break the eggs into a bowl adding salt, pepper, finely chopped herbs, beat everything well, melt some butter in a pan and toss in the beaten. When it takes color, fold on itself and serve immediately.

Then, by turning them without folding them on themselves, but with a plate, and cut into strips. Burrata a pan and scatter a messily first layer of the aforesaid strips.

Sprinkle with parmesan cheese, chopped parsley, pepper, and sprinkle with the excellent tomato sauce; continue the same for four or five layers and on the last layer make a layer of slices of fresh cheese (provolone, mozzarella, graviera, etc.), on which you will sprinkle again with grated gruyere cheese and put small pieces of butter.

Bake to brown on top.

Eggs to drink

Boil water in a quantity that covers them and exceeds them by 0,40 inch. about.

As soon as it boils strongly, adds the eggs, removes the saucepan from the heat, count six minutes, and sort them out by serving them on a towel or in the oven.

Eggs with currie

Melt a piece of butter with flour and a teaspoon of curry

Make the curry with this method:

powder to flavor soups, sauces, soups, etc. It is already prepared in the original English brand saucepans.

It can be easily prepared at home by mixing three-fifths of sweet red pepper, one-fifth of hot peppers (cayenne pepper), and one-fifth of saffron, all well dried and ground. The dose of the cayenne can vary according to its spicy strength and so that of the saffron.

Then, extend slowly and stir continuously with broth, and when you have reduced it to the density of sauce add the hard and sliced eggs.

As soon as they are heated, serve them.

Eye eggs

Spread the butter in small pans or refractory plates and break two eggs for each.

Put on the fire and when the egg white has coagulated, turn over the veil of the same that remained on the red without breaking the latter, which is done with a fork; add salt and pepper and after a little more cooking serve.

Eggs with minced sauce

Cut the hard eggs into quarters, place them on a plate and serve after pouring over a chopped sauce or Hachée.

Make the hachée with this method:

Put a piece of butter, parsley, onion, basil, celery, etc., finely chopped, into a saucepan.

Cook them in a little water, then add a teaspoon of flour dissolved in a cup of water.

When it thickens, add chopped gherkins, salt, and pepper.

Tie up and serve.

Puffed eggs

Eggs 6, 14 of milk, 3 tablespoons of flour, butter 1,8 oz., salt.

Mix the flour with part of the milk, add the egg yolks and beat well adding the rest of the milk and a little salt.

Beat the whites until stiff with more salt and mix everything quickly, pour it into a buttered pan and bake immediately for about 20 minutes.

Serve immediately in the same pan.

Breaded eggs

Hard bread 4,40 lb., 6 eggs, 4 fl. oz. mozzarella, butter 1,8 oz.

Put the hard bread in water and when well moistened, remove the crusts with a knife and squeeze it well.

Melt the butter in a saucepan and put the bread in it, stirring always on the fire.

When well blended, get off the heat and slowly add the mozzarella.

Mix well the first egg and when well homogeneous with the mass add another and so on.

Finally, mix the diced cheese and fry in spoonful.

Dear Reader
I am an emerging writer and, with the sales made from the book, I can continue my studies to publish other books on the subject. I would appreciate an honest review from you.
Join Kimberley Smith newsletter to be informed about new books:
kimb.smith.books@gmail.com
Thanks for your support

Cover by Bluebird Provisions on Pixabay

[Free for commercial use - No attribution required]

Visit the author's page

Write to: kimb.smith.books@gmail.com

OTHER PUBLICATIONS BY KIMBERLEY SMITH:

Raising Chickens For Eggs:

The Beginner's Guide To Building A Chicken-Coop, To Learn How to Raise A Happy Backyard Flock. A Homesteading Solution While You Are At Home

Hydroponic Gardening:

A Detailed Guide on Hydronics to Learn the Principles Behind Gardening and Build a Wonderful System While at Home. Techniques for Your Vegetable Cultivations

Keto Copycat Cookbook Restaurant:

A Keto Diet to Feel Your Best. Easy Recipes for Beginners for All Seasons From Appetizers to Desserts to Reduce Inflammation, Lose Weight, and Heal the Immune System

EASY KETO DESERTS

67 Recipes for Beginners for All Seasons

to Reduce Inflammation, Lose Weight, And Heal the Immune System

A Ketogenic Diet to Feel Your Best